The Technology of Farming

Producing Vegetables

Casey Rand

www.raintreepublishers.co.uk
Visit our website to find out
more information about
Raintree books.

To order:

☎ Phone 0845 6044371
📄 Fax +44 (0) 1865 312263
🖥 Email myorders@raintreepublishers.co.uk

Customers from outside the UK please telephone +44 1865 312262

Raintree is an imprint of Capstone Global Library Limited,
a company incorporated in England and Wales having its
registered office at 7 Pilgrim Street, London, EC4V 6LB
– Registered company number: 6695582

Edited by Abby Colich, Megan Cotugno, and Nancy Dickmann
Designed by Victoria Allen
Picture research by Elizabeth Alexander
Illustrations by Oxford Designers & Illustrators
Originated by Capstone Global Library Ltd
Printed and bound in China by China Translation and Printing
Services Ltd

ISBN 978 1 406 24050 4
16 15 14 13 12
10 9 8 7 6 5 4 3 2 1

British Library Cataloguing in Publication Data
Rand, Casey.
  Producing vegetables. -- (The technology of farming)
  1. Vegetables--Juvenile literature. 2. Vegetable trade--
  Juvenile literature. 3. Agricultural innovations--Juvenile
  literature.
  I. Title II. Series
  635-dc23
A full catalogue record for this book is available from the
British Library.

Acknowledgements
We would like to thank the following for permission to
reproduce photographs: Alamy: pp. 11 (© North Wind Picture
Archives), 18 (© Jake Lyell), 23 (© A.T. Willett), 29 (© Steven
Chadwick), 33 (© AGStockUSA), 40 (© George Impey); The
Art Archive: p. 10 (Eileen Tweedy); Corbis: pp. 13 (© Charles
& Josette Lenars), 15 (© Gerald French), 42 (© Xu Yu/Xinhua
Press); FLPA: p. 39 (Suzi Eszterhas/Minden Pictures); Getty
Images: pp. 8 (The Bridgeman Art Library/Prehistoric), 12
(SSPL), 16 (Mary Evans Picture Library), 20 (PhotoAlto/Laurence
Mouton), 25 (Lisa Kyle Young/Photodisc), 31 (MPI), 41 (Alfred
Eisenstaedt/Time Life Pictures); iStockphoto: p. 26 (© Michael
Lynch); Shutterstock: pp. 5 (© rodho), 7 (© Sergey Peterman),
17 (© ilFede), 21 (© Josef Mohyla), 27 (© Carolina K. Smith,
M.D.), 28 (© GoodMood Photo), 34 (© Kenneth Sponsler).

Cover photograph of transplanting seedlings at an organic,
hydroponic greenhouse reproduced with permission from
Getty Images (Kerry Sherck/Aurora).

Every effort has been made to contact copyright holders
of any material reproduced in this book. Any omissions will
be rectified in subsequent printings if notice is given to the
publisher.

Contents

Some words appear in the text in bold, **like this**. You can find out what they mean by looking in the glossary.

What are vegetables?

You probably know that brussels sprouts, carrots, and spinach are all types of vegetables. Vegetables are something we eat. They are the part of a plant that we can eat. But what makes a vegetable a vegetable? How do vegetables grow? And how do vegetables get from a farm to your kitchen?

A healthy diet

Vegetables are a major part of a healthy diet. Most vegetables contain a lot of vitamins and minerals. They are very good for you. Doctors recommend that you eat five or more portions of fruit or vegetables a day.

Plant food and energy

Vegetables are parts of plants that are good to eat. Vegetable plants grow in **soil**. Soil is made up of tiny pieces of rock and clay, as well as rotted plant and animal remains. Vegetable plants need many things, such as minerals and water, to grow. These things are called **nutrients**. Vegetable plants absorb many nutrients, including water, from the soil in which they are growing.

Like all plants, vegetables capture and store energy from the Sun. They use this energy to make sugars from **carbon dioxide** and water. This process is called **photosynthesis**. The sugars produced during photosynthesis can be used by the plant for energy and to grow. During this process oxygen is released as a waste product. Humans and other animals need oxygen to breathe. Without plants there would be no oxygen available, and animals and humans could not survive.

Vegetable plants get nutrients and water from the soil in which they are planted.

Plants

There are hundreds of thousands of different kinds of plants on the planet. A small number of these plants give us vegetables. Plants have many parts. They have roots, **stems**, leaves, flowers, and seeds. Vegetables could be any of these parts. Carrots are the root of a plant. But not all vegetables are roots. Broccoli is the flower of the plant on which it grows. Potatoes are special parts of a stem. Spinach is the leaves of the plants on which they grow.

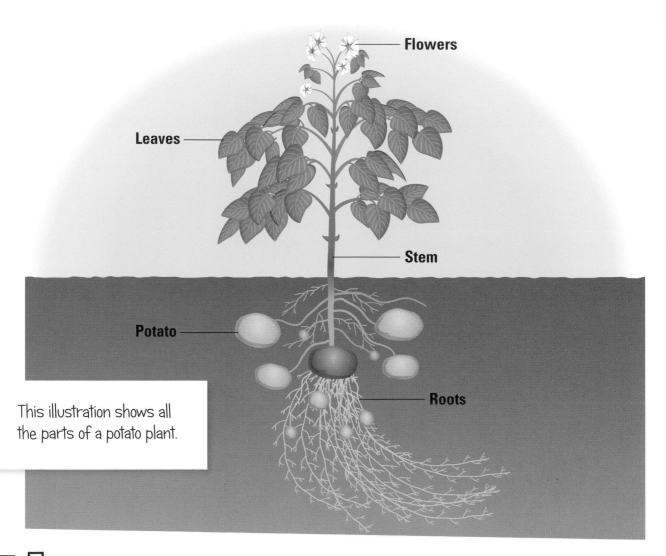

Flowers

Leaves

Stem

Potato

Roots

This illustration shows all the parts of a potato plant.

The tomato contains the seeds of the plant.

Fruit or vegetable?

Not all parts of the plant that can be eaten are vegetables. Fruits are parts of plants, too. Fruits are usually sweeter than vegetables and may be eaten as a dessert. Scientists usually define a fruit as the fleshy part of the plant that surrounds the plant's seeds.

Sometimes deciding if a plant is a fruit or a vegetable is confusing. Something that is classed as a fruit by a scientist may be considered a vegetable by a chef or farmer. For instance, a tomato is considered by most people to be a vegetable. However, since a tomato is the fleshy part of the plant that contains and surrounds the plant's seeds, scientists consider it a fruit. In fact, scientists might say that if you are eating something that contains seeds, you are eating a fruit. So scientists class cucumbers, peppers, corn, peas, and tomatoes as fruits, even though most people consider them vegetables. Neither of these definitions is wrong, and a tomato can be correctly considered both a fruit and a vegetable.

Where do vegetables come from?

You probably eat some type of vegetable every day. If you live in a city, you might wonder where these vegetables come from. If you live in the country, you probably already know that vegetables come from gardens and farms. Farmers and gardeners grow and care for vegetables and pick them when they are ready to eat.

In addition to gathering plants to eat, early humans also hunted their own food.

Hunt and gather

For most of human history, people searched for fruits, vegetables, and nuts that were growing in the wild. These people also hunted animals for food. They were known as **hunter-gatherers**. When they found food, they ate it. When this food was gone, they moved on and began searching for food again. Hunter-gatherers spent most of their day searching for food.

Climate change

While nobody is sure how farming began, historians think it was around 12,000 years ago. At this time the population of humans on Earth began to grow, making finding food more difficult. The **climate** began to change, too. There was hotter weather and less water. This meant there was even less food growing in the wild, and it was even harder to find. Something had to be done.

People began to crowd around areas near rivers, lakes, and other sources of water. In these crowded locations, people could not just walk around and find all the food they needed. This is probably when people started farming so they would have enough food to survive.

Agriculture

Agriculture is the process of producing food by growing certain plants and raising animals, such as cows and sheep. Since everyone needs to eat, agriculture became the centre of most people's lives. People spent most of their days working on the farm to grow and store food for their own use.

More people and more food

Over thousands of years, people started farming more and hunting and gathering less. Farming can support many more people than hunting and gathering can. Farming allowed the human population to grow dramatically.

Jethro Tull

In Britain, farming inventions helped stimulate the agricultural revolution. Jethro Tull may have been the most important inventor of this time. He made improvements to a device called a **seed drill** in 1701. The seed drill was a device pulled by a horse that planted neat rows of seeds.

Jethro Tull believed in using animals for farm work instead of relying on human labour.

The seed drill was much faster than **sowing** the seeds by hand.

Food revolution

For thousands of years after farming began, it stayed mostly the same. Most people worked on farms and grew just enough food to survive. In the 1700s, big changes in farming started to take place. New crops such as corn and potatoes, which were discovered in the Americas, were planted in Europe. New methods of growing vegetables and other foods were developed. New farming tools developed, too. This led to a huge increase in the amount of food produced. This was known as the **agricultural revolution**.

Industrial revolution

In the 1700s, many exciting inventions arrived. These inventions changed agriculture, transport, manufacturing, and almost everything else. Many factories were opened to create the new products that had been invented. People began moving to cities to work in the factories. This was known as the **Industrial Revolution**.

From farm to city

Before the Industrial Revolution, most people lived and worked on farms. As methods of farming improved, more food was produced with less work. This meant fewer workers were needed on the land growing food. Since fewer workers were needed, fewer farming jobs were available. Many families moved to the city for the first time and took jobs in factories.

During the Industrial Revolution. even young children were put to work in the factories.

This Egyptian painting from the 13th century BC shows a husband and wife ploughing a field.

Tools of the trade

The **plough** is a farm tool that has been around for thousands of years. It is pushed or pulled through soil to break up the earth, bury **weeds**, and bring fresh soil to the surface which is better for planting vegetables and other crops. During the 18th and 19th centuries, there were many inventions that greatly improved the plough. A steam-powered plough was invented around 1850. This meant the plough did not have to be pushed by humans or pulled by animals anymore. Steam-powered ploughs were faster, and huge fields could be ploughed very quickly.

How are vegetables produced today?

With new inventions and techniques in the farming of vegetables every year, methods of producing vegetables have changed dramatically since the **Industrial Revolution**. Scientists have found ways to increase the size and amount of vegetables that plants can produce. Engineers have designed bigger and faster farm machines capable of ploughing, planting, and picking huge fields of vegetables more quickly than ever before.

Factory farms

The farms that produce most of the vegetables that people eat today are very large factory farms. These farms are part of something called commercial **agriculture**. Commercial agriculture is the production of crops and animals for distributing and selling on a large scale. These farms produce as much food as possible to make as much money as possible. They use chemicals to help plants grow larger and faster, and they use heavy machines to do the work of farming as quickly as possible.

The world's largest farm is located in Russia and Kazakhstan. This farm grows wheat, corn, and other crops. It is more than 14,760 square kilometres (5,700 square miles) in size.

Large farms, large tractors

Gas-powered tractors today have huge tyres, huge engines, and enormous bodies. The large size is needed since today's farms have grown so big. The world's largest tractors weigh over 45,360 kilograms (100,000 pounds), which is about the same weight as 4 or 5 single-decker buses.

Many farms around the world today have huge fields that stretch as far as the eye can see.

Rotating crops

When the same crop is grown many times in the same field, it depletes the **soil** of various **nutrients**, and the crop no longer grows well. One method that many farmers use to avoid this is **crop rotation**. Crop rotation is the practice of planting different types of crops each season. A farmer might plant beans one year, cabbages the next, potatoes the year after that, and then start the sequence over again. Each plant uses different types and amounts of nutrients from the soil. Rotating the crops gives the soil a chance to replenish nutrients from one year to the next.

Charles Townshend 1675–1738

In England, the four-field system of crop rotation was pioneered by Charles Townshend. He divided his fields into four, planting wheat in the first, clover in the second, oats in the third, and turnips in the fourth. This allowed the fields to rest, increased the nutrients in the soil, and increased the amount of food produced. Townshend soon became known as "Turnip Townshend"!

Charles Townshend spent most of his career as a politician. He had a great interest in agricultural reform.

Export and import

Some countries can only produce certain vegetables during certain seasons. Other countries produce vegetables all year round and then **export** them to countries that cannot grow them. To export means to send and sell a product, such as a vegetable, to another place. Some countries do not have the right weather or soil to grow all the vegetables they need. These countries **import** vegetables (bring in vegetables from other countries).

Giant cargo ships can be used to export vegetables from one country to another.

How are vegetables planted?

Huge fields of vegetables do not just grow by luck. Producing vegetables takes the right kind of **soil**, weather, and care.

In some parts of the world, families still operate small farms to grow enough food for themselves.

Six steps to vegetable success

There are six major steps used today in farming vegetables. Each uses special methods, tools, and machines. You will learn more about each of these steps later in the book.

1. Prepare the soil.
2. Plant the seed.
3. Protect the plant.
4. Feed the plant.
5. Pick the vegetable.
6. Store the vegetable.

The hoe

The hoe is a hand tool that has been around for thousands of years. It can be used to perform multiple gardening functions, such as controlling **weeds** and turning the soil over to prepare for planting seeds.

Preparing the soil

Soil is not just earth. It is a mixture of air, water, minerals, and decaying animals and plants. Some soil is very good for growing vegetables, and some of it is very bad. And different vegetables grow best in different kinds of soil.

Farmers prepare the soil by loosening the top soil and mixing it with lower layers. This helps the soil to hold water and other nutrients better. In gardens and small farms, hand tools such as shovels, **hoes**, and rakes can be used to prepare the soil. **Fertilizers** can also be mixed into the soil before planting vegetables.

Planting the seeds

Most vegetable plants start as seeds. Once the soil is prepared for planting, the seeds of the vegetable plant have to get into the soil. Seeds are not likely to grow well if they are just thrown on top of the soil. Seeds need to be put beneath the top of the soil to protect them from wind, weather, and animals.

Farmers have to dig small holes, put the seeds in these holes, and then cover the seed with more soil. You can imagine this would take a very long time if you were doing it by hand.

Many plants start as seeds, but these potatoes start as tubers – which are sprouting potatoes.

The seed drill allows farmers to sow seeds in just one step. It digs small holes. drops seeds into each. and then covers the seeds with soil.

Seed drill

Seed drills are a **sowing** device. Sowing is a word that means planting seeds. So seed drills are a type of farming tool that helps farmers plant seeds. There are seed drills that can be pushed by hand or pulled by a horse or ox, and there are seed drills that attach to giant tractors for larger jobs.

How do vegetables grow?

Inside every seed is a tiny plant just waiting until the right time to begin to grow. Once the seed of a vegetable plant is in the ground, the tiny plant can break free from the seed and begin to grow. Some seeds will wait until they have water to start to grow, but others prefer to be very dry before growing.

Sun powered

How does a tiny seed as small as your fingernail turn into a giant plant with a pumpkin the size of your head? All seeds have a small amount of stored food inside them. This is what gives the seed energy to start growth. Once the seed begins to grow into a plant, the roots of the seed will capture water and minerals from the ground. The leaves of the plant will capture energy from the Sun and store this energy as sugars.

Weather the storm

One of the most important things a vegetable plant needs to grow is the right weather. Vegetable plants need sunshine and rain to grow. However, some weather can be very bad for farmers. A **drought** can cause plants to dry out and die. A flood can cause plants to drown. Tornadoes can pull plants completely out of the ground. Weather cannot be controlled, so even with the technology that farmers have today, they still are at the mercy of nature.

Tornadoes have the unstoppable power to destroy crops and farm equipment

Feeding the fields

Plants get the **nutrients** they need in order to grow from soil. Soil naturally contains many nutrients, but sometimes it is not enough. Farmers can add **fertilizer** to soil to supply plants with extra nutrients that will help them grow. Fertilizer is another word for plant food. There are two main types of fertilizer used today:

1. **Organic fertilizers** have been used for thousands of years. These fertilizers are composed of naturally occurring materials such as animal manure, seaweed, and dead fish.

2. **Inorganic fertilizers** have only been around for a few hundred years. These fertilizers are human-made substances. While these fertilizers can work well, they can also be hazardous to the environment.

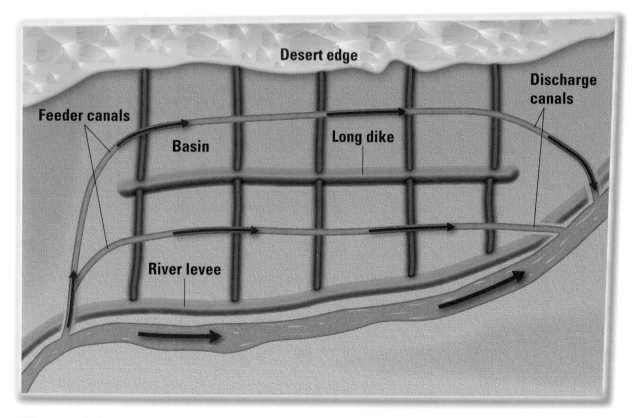

Canals like these used to be dug by hand and allowed water to hydrate the farm fields.

Pivot sprayers can be used to water giant fields of vegetables quickly and efficiently.

Watering the fields

Plants get thirsty, just like you. Plants get most of the water they need from soil. When there is not enough rainfall, farmers find other ways to water the fields. **Irrigation** is the science of getting water into the soil for plants. In ancient Egypt, farmers dug canals that let water from rivers flow into their fields. Today farmers use pipes, hoses, and machines to get water to their crops.

Pivot sprayer

The **pivot sprayer** is a device many farmers use to water their crops today. Pivot sprayers can be small, like the sprinklers many homes use to water their grass. Pivot sprayers can also be huge. These devices make growing crops even in very dry climates possible.

How are vegetables protected?

Once vegetable plants get enough food and water and begin to grow, the farmer's work is not over. There are a lot of insects and animals that would love to eat the farmer's plants. There are also **weeds** that can grow in the farmer's fields and can kill the crops. And just like human beings, plants can catch diseases.

A hornworm is a caterpillar that can eat an entire vegetable plant in just one day!

Crop sprayer

A crop sprayer is usually a small plane that is used to spray a crop field with pesticides or fertilizers. Crop sprayers can do this job much faster than tractors or pivot sprayers.

Crop sprayers have been used since the 1920s to help farmers protect their crops.

Pests and pesticides

Insects and weeds are two of the biggest threats that farmers have to deal with when growing vegetables. Many insects are **herbivores**. Herbivores are organisms that eat plants. Insects eat the leaves, vegetables, flowers, and even the **stems** of plants. Weeds are actually a type of plant. They are unwanted plants that grow in farmers' fields or gardens. Weeds can cause damage to vegetable plants by competing with them for light and **nutrients**, such as water.

Farmers use substances called **pesticides** to try to keep insects and weeds out of their fields. Some pesticides act as a shield to keep insects and weeds away from fields with crops. Other pesticides are meant to kill insects and weeds that are in the field. Pesticides are usually sprayed on to fields using tractors or **pivot sprayers**.

Vegetable attackers from the sky

Of all the animals that threaten a farmer's vegetable fields, birds may be the most dangerous to the crops. Birds feed on the seeds of many vegetable plants and also eat developing vegetable plants. Many farmers try to scare birds away from their fields. To do this, they use loud noises and fake predators. A plastic owl or hawk can be used to scare away other birds and protect the growing plants.

Scarecrow

Are you afraid of scarecrows? A scarecrow is a fake person usually made out of straw, old clothes, and a stick. Many birds are afraid of scarecrows, so farmers use them to keep birds away from their crops. The scarecrow is one of the oldest-known farming tools.

Scarecrows were used more than 3,000 years ago by the ancient Egyptians.

Gardeners often use small fences to keep animals, such as this rabbit, from eating their crops.

Vegetable attackers from the ground

Deer and rabbits are two animals that can threaten vegetable plants on the ground. Deer love to eat leafy crops such as spinach. Rabbits love carrots but will eat almost any vegetables they can find. Some farmers hunt these animals to keep them out of their fields. Others use unusual methods, such as hanging soap in trees because deer do not like the smell of soap.

Some rodents try to get at vegetables from under the ground. These animals make tunnels through farm fields and gardens. They eat the roots of vegetable plants, killing the rest of the plant.

Sick vegetables

Did you know that plants can get ill? Just like humans and other animals, plants are vulnerable to sickness and diseases. These sicknesses and diseases can be carried by organisms in the soil, or even in the water. And just like humans, when plants catch diseases they can make plants around them ill, too. This is especially dangerous in large fields, where plant diseases can spread quickly and ruin entire crops.

Once a plant is diseased, it is difficult to treat, so farmers try to prevent their crops from catching diseases in the first place. They can do this by using crops that are resistant to diseases, or by using chemicals that help the seeds and plants fight against disease.

Luther Burbank
1849–1926

Luther Burbank was an American plant breeder. He was responsible for developing more than 800 new strains of plants including potatoes, various fruits, trees, and flowers. His most famous invention was the Russet Burbank potato. This potato was resistant to many potato diseases, including the one that had caused the Irish Potato Famine.

Irish Potato Famine

Beginning in 1845, a disease called **potato blight** spread across the potato plants in Ireland. At the time, potatoes were a major part of the Irish diet. When the potato crops began to die, many people went hungry. During the **Irish Potato Famine,** approximately one million people in Ireland starved to death.

The Russet Burbank potato, invented by Luther Burbank, helped Ireland recover from the Famine and probably saved many from starvation.

How do vegetables get from the farm to you?

To grow vegetables that are ready to eat, vegetable plants need minerals and water. They have to avoid **droughts**, floods, and other destructive weather. They also have to survive the many predators that would like to eat them before they can fully grow. If they make it this far, it is time for the **harvest**.

Harvesting

The process of picking, cutting, and gathering ripe vegetables is known as harvesting. For much of farming history, harvesting was done by hand. Farmers would use a sharp tool to cut the vegetable from the plant or dig it from the ground. The vegetables were then usually carried in a basket. However, today most harvesting is done using large machines.

Farming machines

Some vegetables, such as cauliflowers and lettuces, grow above the ground. Others, such as carrots and potatoes, grow below ground. Each type of vegetable requires special methods for harvesting. For instance, a huge machine called a lettuce harvester is used to harvest lettuce. This giant machine can harvest as much as 1,360 kilograms (3,000 pounds) of lettuce at any one time!

This John Deere Harvester can greatly reduce the number of hours required to harvest a farm field.

John Deere
1804–1886

American blacksmith, John Deere invented the steel plough in 1837. His invention helped him start The John Deere Company that sells harvesters, ploughs, tractors, and all kinds of agricultural machinery. Today this company is one of the largest producers of agricultural equipment in the world.

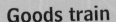

Goods train

The goods train is a type of train used to transport large amounts of cargo. Goods trains are often used to move vegetables from one place to another. They can move a massive amount of vegetables at once.

The heaviest goods train on record weighed 100 million kilograms (220 million pounds) and was more than 7.25 kilometres (4.5 miles) long!

Moving the goods

After vegetables have been **harvested**, they have to be moved from the farm to warehouses for storage and processing, or to shops and supermarkets for sale. Planes, trains, ships, and lorries can all be involved in this process.

Heavy veggie

While some vegetables are easy for farmers to harvest and transport, some are much more difficult. The pumpkin is one of the largest and most difficult vegetables to harvest and transport. Pumpkins normally weigh between 4 and 8 kilograms (9 and 18 pounds) but have been known to grow up to 34 kilograms (75 pounds). Even today many farms have to harvest pumpkins by hand.

Preserving vegetables

Not all vegetables are stored and shipped fresh. Once vegetables are harvested, many of them only have a short life before they begin to go bad. To avoid this, vegetables can be frozen, tinned, or bottled. All of these methods are used to extend the life of the vegetables as a food product. Tinned vegetables have been known to remain edible after more than 100 years. Most fresh vegetables need to be eaten within one week of purchase, although some, such as potatoes and carrots, can be kept for months.

How can producing vegetables help the planet?

Producing vegetables can release oxygen into the air for people to breath, provide healthy food for people to eat, and reduce waste created by raising animals for food. However, producing vegetables can also be bad for the environment if it is not done in the right way.

Vegetables help you breathe

Photosynthesis is the process plants use to make sugars using energy from the Sun. During photosynthesis plants use **carbon dioxide**. Some of this carbon dioxide is made by their cells, and some of it is taken in from the air around the plant. They combine this carbon dioxide, the water their roots absorb, and the sunlight their leaves capture to create sugars. This process releases oxygen back into the air.

The oxygen released during photosynthesis is the oxygen that humans and other animals breathe. Photosynthesis makes life on Earth possible for animals. Before plants began releasing oxygen through this process, there was not enough oxygen on Earth for animals to survive.

Vegetables help you move

Humans need energy to run, jump, or even just to blink. Most of the energy on Earth comes from the Sun. But humans cannot capture energy directly from the Sun. We need plants to do this for us. Humans and all other animals rely on plants to capture the Sun's energy. The sugars created by plants during photosynthesis are what humans use for energy.

Photosynthesis creates sugars that give us energy, and oxygen for us to breathe.

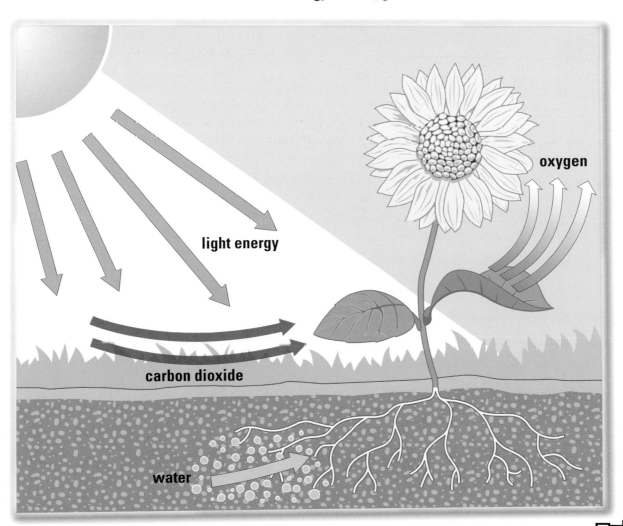

oxygen

light energy

carbon dioxide

water

Climate change

You may have heard of **climate change**. There has been a recent increase in the temperature of Earth's air and water. This increase in temperature has been very small, but even a small increase can have huge consequences for the planet. These changes can cause destructive storms and melting ice caps.

Some of the climate change is being caused by an increase of **greenhouse gases**, such as carbon dioxide, in the air. Burning **fossil fuels** causes the increase in carbon dioxide. Using large farm equipment and transporting vegetables by trains, lorries, and ships contributes to carbon dioxide pollution, too. This increase in carbon dioxide in the air has caused an increase in temperature on Earth.

Plants to the rescue

Plants can play a huge role in reducing the amount of carbon dioxide in the environment. Reducing carbon dioxide in the air can reduce climate change. Photosynthesis gets rid of carbon dioxide from the air. The more plants we have, the more photosynthesis takes place, and the less carbon dioxide there will be.

How you can help

You, too, can play an important role in reducing the amount of carbon dioxide in the environment. Here are a few things you can do:

- Eat locally grown fruits and vegetables.
- Plant trees, flowers, or a vegetable garden.
- Ride your bike to school instead of using a car.

Melting ice caps could cause some animals to lose their icy homes.

Farming can cause erosion through the blowing and washing away of soil from farmlands.

Dirty farming

As the world's population grows, the amount of vegetables and other foods that must be produced grows, too. While new technologies have made producing vegetables easier, they have also had negative environmental side effects.

- Farmers today may use chemical **fertilizers** and **pesticides**. These chemicals can get into water supplies and be absorbed into the vegetables we eat.

- Vegetable production can also cause **soil erosion** through tilling. Tilling is the process of preparing soil for planting vegetables. Tilling loosens the soil. Loose soil can blow away in the wind or wash away in rain. This is called soil erosion.

- Use of large farm equipment causes an increase in carbon dioxide emissions.

Sustainable farming

Sustainable farming means finding ways to produce enough vegetables and food for everyone without hurting the environment. One method of sustainable farming is **organic farming**. Organic farmers replace chemical fertilizers and pesticides with more natural and environmentally friendly methods, such as using manure from animals. Organic farmers also rely on **crop rotation** to reduce their need for fertilizers.

Rachel Carson
1907–1964

Rachel Carson was an American scientist who helped make people aware of the dangers of using some chemical pesticides. DDT is a pesticide that became popular with farmers in the 1940s. Carson showed that DDT negatively affects many animals in the environment. Her book *Silent Spring* was a key factor in the banning of DDT in the 1970s and 1980s by governments around the world.

Rachel Carson is pictured here in 1962.

How has vegetable production changed the world?

When humans were mostly hunters and gatherers, people had to work constantly to find food. Because there was a limited amount of food, it was not always easy to find. The development of farming allowed vegetable and food production to increase dramatically, changing the way people lived forever.

Life on Earth

Plants, such as vegetable plants, are constantly releasing oxygen into the air and storing the Sun's energy. This oxygen and energy are what make life on Earth possible for humans and animals. Without plants humans could not survive on Earth.

While the world around us continues to change, vegetables remain a healthy part of both the environment and the human diet.

Vegetable time

The farming of vegetables and other foods meant that the human population increased dramatically. Farming allowed food to be found easily, so humans did not have to search for it anymore. This meant that people could use their time for things besides finding food, such as education, arts, and writing.

Improved production

There are six major steps in producing vegetables:

1. Prepare the soil.
2. Plant the seed.
3. Protect the plant.
4. Feed the plant.
5. Pick the vegetable.
6. Store the vegetable.

Improvements and new technologies have allowed each of these steps to be done more quickly and efficiently. This has led to massive increases in vegetable production.

Saving the planet

While modern farming has found ways to produce more plants, including vegetables, it has also harmed the environment through the use of chemicals and through **soil erosion**. Scientists and farmers are working together to find ways to make farming more sustainable.

Glossary

agricultural revolution increase in agricultural productivity between the 17th and 19th centuries due to improved techniques and new technology. It is also sometimes called the green revolution.

agriculture farming

carbon dioxide gas produced as a waste product during respiration in the cells. It is used during photosynthesis in plants to create sugars with oxygen as a waste product.

climate usual conditions of the weather, including temperature, precipitation, and wind

climate change slow change in temperature of Earth's surface air and water caused by increases in greenhouse gases in the air

crop rotation successive planting of different crops on the same land to improve soil fertility and help control insects and diseases

drought long period of time without enough rain

export to send goods or materials abroad for trade or sale

fertilizer natural or human-made materials used to increase the nutrients in soil used for farming

fossil fuels fuel that is formed within Earth from plant or animal remains

greenhouse gas any gas in the atmosphere, such as carbon dioxide or methane, that traps heat

harvest gathering of a crop

herbivores organisms that eat only plants

hoe farming tool with a flat blade used for weeding, cultivating, and gardening

hunter-gatherer person who hunts and searches for food in the wild

import to bring in goods or materials from abroad for trade or sale

Industrial Revolution period between the 18th and 19th centuries in which new technology led to major changes in society

inorganic fertilizer fertilizer made from human-made materials

Irish Potato Famine famine in Ireland caused by a disease of the potato crop

irrigation science of getting water to the soil for plants

nutrient substance that the body needs to grow and function

organic farming farming done using natural materials and methods

organic fertilizer fertilizer made from natural materials

pesticide chemical used to kill pests, such as insects

photosynthesis process by which plants combine carbon dioxide and water to make sugar and oxygen. They use energy from the Sun captured by special cells in their leaves.

pivot sprayer farming tool used to water crops by spraying water

plough farm tool used for breaking up soil and preparing the soil for planting seeds

potato blight disease that strikes and kills potatoes. Potato blight caused the Irish Potato Famine in the 1840s.

seed drill farming tool or machine that plants seeds and covers them with soil

soil top layer of Earth's land surface, consisting of rock and mineral particles mixed with organic matter

soil erosion wearing away of topsoil through wind or rainwater

sow to scatter or plant seeds in the ground

stem stalk or trunk of the plant

sustainable farming using methods of farming that both produce crops and are safe for the environment

weed unwanted plant that grows in farmers' fields or gardens

Find out more

Books

Earth-Friendly Food (How to be Earth Friendly), Gillian Gosman (Powerkids Press, 2011)

Farming for the Future (Planet SOS), Gerry Bailey (Gareth Stevens Publishing, 2011)

Farming Vegetables and Grains (Ethics of Food), Michael Burgan (Raintree, 2011)

Food for Life (Sustainable Futures), John Bains (Evans Brothers Ltd, 2012)

Local Farms and Sustainable Foods (Save the Planet), Julia Vogel (Cherry Lake, 2010)

Vegetables, Louise Spilsbury (Heinemann Library, 2010)

Websites

UK Agriculture

An interactive website that allows you to explore the history and development of the British countryside, farming, and agriculture – from the Ice Age to the present time!

www.ukagriculture.com/countryside/countryside_history.cfm

The Soil Association

This website explains the aims of the Soil Association, and provides information and news on organic farmers and farming practices. It also has a list of organic farms in the United Kingdom that welcome visitors.

www.soilassociation.org

Eco-Friendly Kids

Visit this website to discover some tips on how you can become more eco-aware – and how you could grow your own fruit and veg!.

www.ecofriendlykids.co.uk/FoodCategory.html

Family Learning

Find out more about the importance of eating a balanced diet – and why this should include plenty of fruit and vegetables.

www.familylearning.org.uk/5-a-day.html

Places to visit

Museums

There are many local museums of rural life that give you a good idea of farming practices in the past. You can find your nearest museum by searching on the internet.

www.britainsfinest.co.uk/museums/search_results.cfm/searchclasscode/435

Farmers' markets

Use the website below to find a farmers' market near you. At many farmers' markets, you can talk to farmers who might be able to tell you more about their farming practices.

www.local-farmers-markets.co.uk

Agricultural shows

A great way to see farm animals and all the latest farm machinery is to visit an agricultural show. These shows often have livestock competitions and other agricultural events as well. Check on the internet to find a show near you that welcomes visitors.

Index